Sinner,

Turned

Role Model,

Turned

Advocate

Revised Edition

Roderick D. Talley

ISBN: 978-1-7342540-8-2 (print)
      978-1-957294-03-2 (ebook)

R.D. Talley Books Publishing, LLC
4882 W. Lone Mountain Rd.
Las Vegas, Nevada 89130
www.rdtalleybooks.com

I would like to thank God for guiding, inspiring, and providing strength for my journey throughout my life.

I would also like to thank my friends, family, and my wonderful queen, Ebony, for your support and encouragement that helpedshape this book.

A special thank you goes to Professor Zachary Locklin for helping to reignite my passion for poetry.

Lord, I pray that this book helps each and every person who reads it, no matter what their beliefs are. Please speak to their hearts. Give them peace of mind and comfort in whatever situation they are currently dealing with. Let them know that you are in control of everything. In Jesus's name we pray, Amen.

Prologue

I am and will continue to be living proof that your past mistakes do not dictate your future. You are not a mistake just because of your past mistakes.

It took several years before I fully grasped and believed the statement above, but once I did, I knew I had to spread this knowledge. I realized that God still had a purpose for my life, despite my mistakes and shortcomings. In fact, I later learned that He wanted to use those same mistakes and shortcomings to get the glory out of my life.

The same goes for you, my fellow kings and queens. I want you to know that God loves you unconditionally, no matter how bad your mistakes may have been. God loves you and still has a purpose for your life. I encourage you all to take hold of this truth and ask God to guide you from now on. Be that beacon of hope who went from a careless sinner, to a positive role model, to a firm advocate for Jesus Christ!

God bless you and enjoy!!

Contents

Living Proof

It was sworn by my 5th grade teacher
that I wouldn't amount to anything,
According to statistics, I was destined to be either dead,
in jail, or stuck with some kind of disease

And yes, I've served time in jail before
but I believe there's a lesson in every mistake,
and I refused to let my future go to ruins
just because of my past mistakes

I made it a goal to improve myself daily
and I quickly learned that I needed God's helping hand,
I realized that I needed his guidance, his grace
and his covering in order to become a real man

I learned how to persevere through the trials & tribulations of life,
worked my butt-off to become a deserving husband for my wife,
and over the years I've gradually become living proof
that God can make the best out of anyone's life.

Old Yet New News

Just received word earlier today
that one of my childhood friends' life was taken by gunfire
the continued violence in Cincinnati
was the primary reason my relocation from there was inspired
The funny thing is that I haven't heard from him in years
yet I thought of him and his family just last week
I know quite a few people in whom I grew up with
that have passed away since I left Ohio,
but this one hits closer to home . . .
Some of my first fighting lessons came from this man,
lessons of the importance of family came from him too…
My mother reminisced joyful memories of our childhood together
as she brought me the bad news
ironically, shootings have become normal news in that city…
I heard you left behind four beautiful daughters
and I hope we'll get to meet them one day…
I also hope that you found Christ,
If so, a small part of me is glad that you're in a better place
I send my condolences to your mother, Gabrea,
your brother, Jason, your sisters, Erica & Kelly
At thirty years of age, you were too young to make an exit
I'm sorry we couldn't meet up
and share some crazy laughs again…
Farewell, my brother, Mr. Camrin Starr.

Flashbacks Pt. 1

(Free Verse)

As I cruise down I-405 I think a bit of how far I've come . . .
The chipped-tooth & dirty clothes gave fuel to my anger,
the back-stabbing "friends" I kept close
created more distance with me and my family.
I could steal items from under anyone's nose
and deceive them to believe that they misplaced it...
The label of a problem-child I strongly resembled.
I even deserted my brothers for the sake of fitting-in the crowd.
My heavy-handed fists helped me fight my way out of
any sticky matter,
with no regards to how bad the other person got hurt...
It was crazy how talented I was at all the wrong things.

Then my light switch was flipped somehow.
The same Three-Six Mafia & Tupac music I allowed
to influence my train of thought and
all the actions I used to take is playing in my car right now . . .
except now I no longer hold it in high regards—*at all!*
They can't even scratch the surface of my spirit anymore. Moments
like this, I feel like Frederick Douglass-
refusing to allow my mind, body, & spirit
to continue being enslaved by my environment . . .
Just a small sign that God is still working on me.
Thank you, Lord, for everything.

Blessed

I think back on all the things I've been through,
the problems I've run into,
the things I used to do . . .
I figured that my life is such a mess
and there are so many issues that I need to correct.

Then I think back on all the things that's been right,
the caring people in my life,
the problems I've made right . . .
I think back and realize there was always a helping hand,
and I realize how blessed I am.

Definition—The Lack Of

(Free Verse)

They say that time is money,
as if you can buy yourself peace and freedom . . .
But if that's the case then I'm doing something wrong
because my bank account sits comfortably in three digits
yet it's not enough to free this headache
and it remains imprisoned in my dome-
It pounds my skull day and night attempting to break free
and move on . . .

I'm sickened to learn how heroine claimed the life
of another person I knew...
Someone who just couldn't kick the habit-
Dang I wish my advising words would've sunk through.

My friend is still serving life in prison for murder...
Can't fathom what he's going through.

They say that time is money, ironically you can't buy back time,
can't go back and change decisions
there's no refunds, no take-backs, no next-times

I become even more sickened
when I hear the garbage on the radio
boasting about their borrowed money,
their unauthorized rights to call women b****** & h***,

bragging about their over-priced clothes
from designers who aren't going to pay them a dime though quick
to announce they're selling drugs,
yet slow to realize they're only "federal thugs"
They've clearly never seen a whole neighborhood
strung-out on drugs—
Talk about a Nightmare on Elm Street.

I wish these radio gangsters would speak on
something beneficial,
Something with some definition
instead of the misdirected, arrhythmic, meaningless trash
they write with no substance,
and help create a structured and uplifting form . . .
But our society remains divided and unformed,
just like this poem.

Normal Mornings

(Everyday Poem)

Left shoe, right shoe, now I'm fully dressed
I lean over the bed to kiss my queen before departing
She grins, mumbles, "I love you", then falls right back to sleep
I'm quite the early-bird but she thinks 8:00 a.m.
is too early for anything
I walk into the living room and grab the Walmart list
as well as my keys, wallet, phone, pen, and ChapStick
I take-in the scene of our home and its cleanliness.

Walk outside to unlock our black Trailblazer
and check myself in its clean reflection
Pull out to the alley and see a man standing a few feet away
Carries himself like a so-called "dope-dealer"
but I remain pleasant-
Offered to say a quick prayer for him
but he confusingly declined
Hop back in the truck and glance at the sky
as I roll my windows down
Put my shades & seatbelts on as I turn onto Cherry Ave.,
The sunshine and cool breeze reminds me of how far I've come-
and helps remind me to stay humble.

Get to Walmart and park next to a pearl-white Benz,
the trunk opens as I cut the engine,
and an attractive woman approaches the Benz
Being the courteous person I am, I get out, smile and nod . . .
She smiles and winks . . . then bites her lips …
My wife always warned me to watch how I show the dimples . . .
I wave at her with my left hand
so she'll have a great view of my wedding band,
Continue to enter the lively marketplace,
although I'm happily off the market.

Gratitude

Every now and then, I think back
on all the tests you've brought me through
And it feels border-line disrespectful
for me not to express any gratitude

I don't praise you for any personal gain
Nor do I do it to get anything in return
Lord, I praise you because I'm still thankful
for the lessons those hardships made me learn

You've gradually built my character over time,
I'm a much-better man than I used to be,
Thanks to you, I've become a light in the darkness
mentally, physically, socially, and spiritually

I've known for quite some time now
That you've been making a difference
in my life, as well other people's lives,
but now, even other people see the difference

You bled and died on that cross for our sins,
making this transformation in me possible,
I just want to thank you for residing in my life,
helping me to become something out of the impossible.

Fall From Power

(Blank Verse)

When it rains it pours, you know you've messed-up
you've been in this battle far too long now
you want to keep this a secret but can't
too much exposure of this will hurt too
too much pride at stake, too much brass to lose
too many lives have already been hurt
too many lies have already been told
too many years of bobbing and weaving
too much of people's trust have been betrayed
now the seeds you've sown are starting to reap
the pressure has built beyond containment
your dark, heartless schemes have been brought to light everyone
you've helped has turned against you
your mighty towers are now crashing down
you ask, "Is this what it all boils down to?"
But you decided to learn the hard way.

Inmate # ----

(Narrative Poem)

They grip the handcuffs tight around my wrists
yet they're soothing hands caress my forearms
as they walk me to the patrol car.
The older lady officer finally seems to relax
as she gets into the driver's seat, and her
younger partner calmly tells me that I should be out
shortly after they turn in their arrest report,
But I received the colored wristband for felons during processing
and then was locked-in on the fifth floor of the jailhouse
with the gang members, domestic abusers,
and other felonious offenders,
Just one floor under the murderers and rapists . . .
Darn, those women tricked me.
I admitted my wrong in signing the money order
How the heck was I supposed to know it was fake?!
I allowed the building-pressure of financial restrictions
and the falsely reassuring words
of two lady cops get the best of me…
That's the last time I would let any deceitful woman or cop
gain my trust.

I knew I had to pay the consequences and roll with the punches
but I didn't know they were going to hit me this hard . . .
Roll call five times a day,
Cold sandwiches each meal every day
due to the kitchen being under renovations,
Limited time to take showers and watch TV,
Lock-down for nearly one third of every day,
No one to call on the phone
because my family are all far away
and the inmate phones won't allow long-distance calls,
No clear view of outdoors,
You could only hear the sounds of freedom
through a high-window in the rec yard area,
Contraband searches at random times,
My wrists and feet were bound in cuffs and chains
for the first three days of my stay . . .
They really do strip you of your freedom while confined.

My first request for release got rejected without consideration
and my arraignments didn't go well either.
My anger was flaming for the first three days.
I felt like a nuclear bomb ready to explode and create chaos
for being so stupid; me punishing myself for ending up in here.
But there was something about day number four
that helped me switch my mindset.
The quote, "Everything happens for a reason"
crossed my mind and I began speaking to God—
And I don't mean in tongues either.
I let out all my emotion at Him
and asked for the reason of this phase,
then it hit me a couple of days later while reading the Bible—
He had to get my attention.

I began praying and asking for forgiveness and guidance.
I even prayed for a couple of other inmates too.
I asked God to teach me how to see through the fog
when life's situations try to clog my mind and distract me.
It was easy to stay focused in jail
because there was nothing else to do,
but I knew that I needed help
once I was released back into the world
where distractions come from any and every direction.
After fourteen days of confinement, I was released
and after approximately ninety days
my felony was reduced to a misdemeanor.
No bail money. No one's help. No schemes.
It was just God letting me know that He's all I need
and that I need to place my trust in Him
instead of my own abilities.
I've been trusting Him ever since.

I'm Not Afraid

Dear Jesus,
I want you to know that I pledge allegiance to the purpose you died
on the cross for
I've had to fight adversity my whole life,
so I'm not a stranger to war
The difference now is that I fight
with a clearer view and sense of direction
Years ago, I was fighting while under fear,
but now I know that I have your protection
Enlist me into your army, Lord,
at least I know that I won't be deceived by you
Although I received an honorable discharge from the armed forces,
hardly anything about their intent and purpose
seemed honorable and true
Put me in the fight, Lord,
you can place me on the front-line if you choose to
I believe you died for my sins,
therefore, I'm willing and ready to lay down my life for you
Too many people are troubled and need to know of your existence,
Too many people need your guidance,
protection, and your comfort at this instance
You've proven to me many times that you're worth my trust
and I'll follow you into the depths of hell, if I must
I know that I'm far from perfect and still make a lot of mistakes
but you've shown on countless occasions
that I'm covered with your grace

I'm not afraid to live and die for you, Lord,
so use me to share your love to this dying world
Use me to help other people see you through me,
so they'll know there's hope beyond this world

Holiday Surprise

Through the 1985-style door,
I'm welcomed to a display of radiant décor . . .

Mini-prickly reefs hang above each window
each reef with golden bells and red-ribbon bows
A red furry blanket hangs over the couch
two white pillows with golden swirls that go about
in continuous circles and a red pillow sits in between,
the dining table is set with a Christmas theme.
In the kitchen more reefs hang atop the wooden cabinet doors,
ornaments and hand-made decorations
sit on the brown carpet floor
Her four-foot, seven-inch frame jitters with excitement
as she anticipates my response…
A live pine tree would fit well near the front.

Dope "Game"

All of your options will be limited,
Constant paranoia is what you'll be dealing with
Yeah, you may see some money come fast
but that's about the only so-called benefit

Yet, if the truth be told,
The cons far outweigh the pros
and all the things that come with that fast money
deliver deadly and life-crippling back-blows

Do yourself a favor,
Take a step back
and look at it from a bigger view . . .

Selling drugs is called a "game"
because the outcomes have always been the same . . .
you end up either stripped of your freedom in jail,
strung-out on the streets, or slain

The people involved
get paid from helping other people's brains dissolve,
The reason the money comes fast is because
the dealer's souls also quickly dissolve

Most who go into the "game" die young,
They allow themselves to be used as pawns
instead of developing into the kings and queens
that God has called them to be upon

Satan wants you to be confused and destroyed
Some "rappers" are being used to play with your mind like a toy
If they don't mention the dark side of selling drugs in their songs,
Please read between the lines
and recognize they're presenting a ploy

God has much-bigger purposes for your lives,
Not wanting you to live in bondage from believing in lies
Instead of destroying his most valued creations in humans
He wants you to help empower other people's lives.

> *The thief does not come except to steal, and to kill, and to destroy.*
> *I have come that they may have life,*
> *and that they may have it more abundantly.*
> *—John 10:10, NIV*

Preacher's Dilemma

(Petrarchan Sonnet)

Go ahead, tap into the temptation
It surrounds you more and more every day
begging you to take a break and go play . . .
just a break from the daily rotation,
the normal family-life situation
your name's constantly on bigger display
dames smile from the motel across the way
Lord knows sex sells, such a contemplation

For a moment of fun, is it worth it?
You'll lose family trust, respect lost as well
The honor stamped to your name will be stripped
Lord knows that we all are far from perfect
The road back will be harder than you fell
Stay the course, please don't let yourself get tripped.

This Joy

The joy that you have,
the world didn't give it to you & the world can't take it away . . .
unless you allow it.

The nature of the human flesh is to be negative
and people who choose to stay in negativity
will try to discourage all positive energy . . .
Misery truly loves company.

But if you change your mentality
and put your effort into being positive,
then you will discover changes in every aspect of your life.

Hard times will hit us hard,
but what doesn't kill us makes us stronger
It's not an easy transition,
but it's more than worth it . . .

It's worth the brighter perception that you'll have on life,
It's worth the daylight-smile you'll bring to someone's dark-night
It's worth the higher value you will impose on yourself
It's worth you knowing
that your worth doesn't include material wealth

It's worth you treating yourself as the king and queen you are
It's worth you having a positive impact on people,
both near you and afar
It's worth you knowing that God views you as his precious child
So go ahead—be free, be happy, and live a little while.

Modern Times

(Free Verse)

It's funny how our country is the "land of the free"
Yet we're still enslaved by racism, diseases, poverty,
injustice, anger, depression, stress, greed, hatred,
fear, inequality-both financially and physically,
deception, conflict, abuse, confusion, and so-forth.

Lord, help our country.
Better yet, help our world.
Guide our leaders.
Help all of us persecuted people be a light in the darkness,
despite the trials we're enduring-
both domestically and internationally.
I thank you in advance. Amen.

WMD

(Villanelle)

The breaking point is closing-in,
The point of No-Return is near,
My options hover in the wind.

Their threatening words are cutting-in,
The abuse of their rank instills fear,
The breaking point is closing-in.

My tolerance is stretched beyond thin,
Their plot to destroy me is clear,
My options hover in the wind.

They continue pushing me to the brim,
The crowd's anxious silence grazes my ear,
My breaking point is closing-in.

As I ponder where I'll be at today's end,
Something causes the tension to veer,
My options remain in the wind.

They'll get to see their families again,
Higher authorities have interfered,
The breaking-point stops closing-in,
My options vanish in the wind.

Love Avenues

I love discovering that the scriptures written in the Bible are true
because this scripture surely applies to you . . .
The Lord had this scripture in mind while he was creating you,
The Lord knew you would captivate my heart
before I even approached you.
I fell in love with everything about you,
it was much more than just physical attraction,
you stimulated all of my senses
before we even took part in any physical action
You constantly set-off fireworks inside my mind
far before intercourse became intertwined
in our numerous avenues of love expressions . . .

YOU MAKE LOVE TO ME IN SO MANY WAYS, MY QUEEN...

You make love to me with the smile you share
whenever you see me,
your support of my decisions shows how much
you love the spirit in me,
You make love to me when you talk to me with respect,
you make love to me when you take strides with me
without fear or regret,
You make love to me when you pray for me throughout the day,
more love is made when we talk to each other about our days-
and how they went, as well as every time we hold hands…
you make love to me when you encourage me
on being a Godly man…

The love shows as I become more and more ready to fight
anyone who has something negative to say about your height…
Yet that same love calms me down as you remind me
that everything is alright.
I love and appreciate everything about you my virtuous queen…
I pray that it continues to grow to the point
where it's contagiously seen
by everyone who comes within our vicinity.

The Nature of the Flesh

Lord, I really need your help with staying focused on you
because the more I learn about you,
the more I realize how the nature of the flesh
is to keep us as distant from you as possible...

Quite frankly, this explains a lot . . .

This explains why a life of sin is much more attractive than a life of
following your plan,
This explains why we're quick to trust our abilities rather than
placing our issues in your hands,
This explains why some women seek pleasure
from people outside of their husbands,
This explains why some men lust
after their wife's friends and cousins,
This explains why being a Christian is much harder
than being a sinner,
Leading many Christians to concede back to the life of the sinner,
On top of that, Satan makes it easy to trade riches for your soul
opposed to enduring the sufferings of trials
to naturally enrich your soul
Our flesh tends to look at and believe the negative-side of things
The nature of the flesh tends to make us underestimate our ability
Our flesh tends to make us become discouraged somewhat easily
instead of focusing on the fact
that God has already given us the victory

I recognize that the nature of the flesh is to be rebellious
against your purpose
The enemy uses this to trick us into trusting our flesh,
even though it will hurt us
Lord, *please* help us Christians to continue looking past our flesh,
and help us to stay focused on your purpose.

No Comparison

I could be like some people
and brag about the dollar amount in my bank
but the God I serve owns all of earth's money,
both in and out of the bank
I could stand here and talk about how
my life's decisions have made me better than you
but it was really by the strength and grace of God
that I was able to make it through
I could boast about how I'm destined to be a king,
and that my light shines like a candle
but Christ came to earth as the King of Kings,
yet he served the people and he led by example
I could talk about my life achievements,
many of which has earned me a round of applause
yet they don't compare to what Jesus achieved
when he bled for our sins and died on that cross
I've been blessed with a beautiful home,
late-model cars, and other "finer things"
and I could boast and brag about them, but here's the thing:
Most of those "finer things" can't be sold
for more than you brought them for,
In fact, most of those things begin to lose value
as soon as you step outside the retailer's door
A brand-new car depreciates as soon as you drive it off the lot
however, God placed a "priceless" tag on your soul,
meaning that you can't be bought

So why do we look to things of diminishing value to represent our worth?

The point is, we must remember that we're nothing without Christ.
We must remain humble and realize
we're no better than any other human being-
no matter how much we've gained in this life.

I am the vine, you are the branches. If you remain in me and I in you, you will bear much fruit; apart from me you can do nothing. (John 15:5, NIV)

We do not dare to classify or compare ourselves with some who commend themselves. When they measure themselves by themselves and compare themselves with themselves, they are not wise. (2 Corinthians 10:12, NIV)

For it is by grace you have been saved, through faith—and this is not from yourselves, it is the gift of God—not by works, so that no one can boast. (Ephesians 2:8–9, NIV)

Angel On Earth

Aunt Tonia . . .
I want to thank you and Jesus for gracing this planet with your
presence.

Words . . .
They can't express the effect you had on all the people you came in
contact with.

Your smile . . .
The joy of the Lord within you shined through it, sharing it with all
in your vicinity.

Your positive mindset . . .
Was contagious to most people around you, causing us to look-up
to you.

Your wisdom . . .
Your few words brought light to my perspective on family, women
and marriage.

Your love & support . . .
Proved to be the primary adhesive agents that helped keep the
family bonded.

Your presence . . .
Although it's back in heaven, it will be deeply missed here on earth
by many.

The Comeback

(Sestina-Inverted)

His co-workers celebrate the company's latest accomplishment
yet he can't muster the mood to accompany them genuinely
because the only thing that's on his mind is his children,
his true support system, in whom he longs for the day
he will be able to have them again. He thinks to himself,
Lord, please give me strength. Any day now . . . any day now . . .

The divorce left his mind scrambled but he's thinking clearly now
He knows regaining custody would be his ultimate accomplishment
The mother's been disrespectful yet he knows he can't lose himself
He can't deny that deep in his heart, he still loves her genuinely
although he caught her sharing their love with someone else--such a
dreadful day
but he can't let those memories take-over; must stay focused on the
children.

It's Friday and he's excited about spending the weekend with his
children
Every two weeks he gets to see them and it's been two years now
since the divorce became final. Yet, still not a day
goes by that he doesn't consider the births of them
his happiest accomplishments
He looks forward to making sure that they know he loves and
appreciates them genuinely
and he loves how looking in their faces is like seeing
reflections of himself.

As he pulls into his ex-wife's driveway he prepares and braces
himself
for the chaos she creates for him every time he comes to pick up
the children
The kids cover their ears as she continuously curses him genuinely
It's gotten worse over time; even her lover joins in
on the insults now
Spatting out all his failures yet never mentioning his
accomplishments
but he doesn't respond. He just thinks to himself,
Soon, it will be my *day.*

After much stress and preparation, the calendar finally approaches
the day
in which the courtroom awaits his presence. Before entering he
prays by himself
and asks God to help him keep his cool despite the failure or
accomplishment
that may transpire today. He's welcomed by the smiles of his
children
when he walks in the room. He feels much better now
that he sees their brightened faces and as they continue to wave
genuinely.

The judge must've noticed how they deeply connected genuinely
because it didn't take her long before ordering the switch of
custody, effective that day.
The father couldn't believe the amount of weight that was lifted
now
The emotion swelled up inside of him and he couldn't help himself
But to fall on his knees in tears, thanking God, and he was soon
embraced by the hugs of his children . . .

He finally reached his most prized accomplishment.
Now he genuinely thanks God every day
and made a vow to himself
to never let anything separate them,
and that he'll always be there to watch his children
grow into adults and assist in celebrating their accomplishments.

Message To Our Unborn Children

I dream of the day when you beautiful knuckle-heads become a
reality
We've been working overtime to ensure we'll be the best mommy
and daddy
that we can be, when y'all get here, you'll see
We've been working toward living lifestyles that are more healthy
We've created a loving and peaceful environment
that ensures our safety
Sometimes it seems like your mother and I
fell in love almost effortlessly
God made her just for me, and I thank God for her daily
We learned a lot while being raised from our original families
Now we seek to begin our own sustainable legacy
By raising and teaching you to be strong,
both in teams and independently
By teaching you Godly values
and the importance of acting responsibly
By showing you the high value of your worth
yet presenting yourselves humbly
By building you to become strong adults physically and mentally
By giving you the tools to thrive socially and financially
By teaching you from the mistakes we've made in hopes that you'll
take heed
And do the same when you grow older and plant your own seeds
We won't be perfect, but know that we'll give
our maximum effort daily
To show our love and support to you
and grow into a strong family.

9 781734 254082